EASY & ENGAGING ESL ACTIVITIES AND MINI-BOOKS FOR EVERY CLASSROOM

Terrific Teaching Tips, Games, Mini-Books & More to Help New Students From Every Nation Build Basic English Vocabulary and Feel Welcome!

by Kama Einhorn

SCHOLASTIC
PROFESSIONAL BOOKS

New York ✱ Toronto ✱ London ✱ Auckland

Sydney ✱ Mexico City ✱ New Delhi ✱ Hong Kong

For Matty —
Ya yablyu, in any language.

THIS LAND IS YOUR LAND words and music by Woody Guthrie. TRO (c) Copyright 1956
(renewed) 1958 (renewed) 1970 Ludlow Music, Inc., New York, New York. Used by permission.

Edited by Louise Orlando
Cover design by Norma Ortiz
Interior design by Elizabeth Chinman
Illustrations by Cary Pillo

ISBN 0-439-15391-3
Copyright © 2001 by Kama Einhorn
All rights reserved.
Printed in the U.S.A.

Contents

Introduction

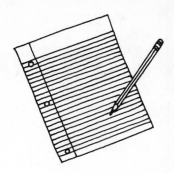

"In New York in school everything happened in English. Such a lonely language. Each letter stands alone and makes its own noise. Not like Chinese..."
— Mei Mei, newcomer student in *I Hate English* by Ellen Levine

The number of children in our schools who are new to the United States is growing. Estimates range from 2.5 million to 4.6 million children (7 to 10 percent of the population), representing more than 180 different language groups. They leave a variety of environments in their home countries and arrive with a whole set of culturally based values and expectations. Most of all, they are scared and anxious about surviving in a new school with a new language.

Supporting second-language learners in a class full of fluent English speakers can seem a daunting task. How will your new students follow the English-language lessons? How will you assess these students? Communicate with the new families? Help the students fit into the group socially? And, most immediately, if you don't share the students' first language and they don't speak any English, how will you communicate throughout the day?

This guide gives you quick and easy ways to provide your second-language learners with a little shelter from the storm. Mini-books, games, and activities help students build a basic English vocabulary and manage their own language-learning experience. From the first day in the classroom, students will complete challenging yet achievable tasks that teach words they need to know immediately. Later on, they will memorize basic texts, such as "The Pledge of Allegiance," that their English-speaking peers know by heart.

Creating a comfortable environment for newcomers who are communicating in a new language is a big job. Use this book as a key resource. Remember, your students' language proficiency will continue to grow as they blossom into active, engaged learners.

TERMS YOU SHOULD KNOW

Following is a list of important terms for teachers with second-language learners. For more information, resources, and ESL policies, check with your school district, as well as your local and state departments of education. You will also find a list of additional resources at the end of this book (page 62).

ESL (English as a Second Language) is a program specifically designed to teach English to non-English speakers. The goal is for learners to achieve greater proficiency in academic and social language. ESL is also called English Language Development (ELD).

ESL Pull-Out Students spend most of each day in a regular classroom. They are "pulled out" on a regular basis to receive special help with English as well as additional support with understanding the classroom curriculum.

Bilingual Education takes several different forms. All are designed to help second-language learners continue to develop grade-level skills in their first language as they acquire English. Bilingual educators use both the students' native language and English in instruction. As instructors do this, they help maintain the new students' self-esteem and pride in their first language and culture. In a *transitional bilingual program,* students spend one to three years in a bilingual class before they are "mainstreamed" into an English-only situation. In a *maintenance bilingual program,* primary-language instruction is provided throughout the elementary grades, so students will become thoroughly bilingual.

Newcomer Programs serve foreign-language students in an environment devoted solely to the social, academic, and cultural adjustment of new immigrants. A newcomer program is comprised only of students who are new to the United States; it emphasizes systematic English-language instruction. A student typically spends only one year in a newcomer program.

Sheltered English or **Specially Designed Academic Instruction in English (SDAIE)** uses English to teach the normal grade-level curriculum while using second-language learning techniques that foster academic and linguistic development.

Structured English Immersion is immersion in a totally English-speaking environment without native-language support or instruction. The curriculum is taught entirely in English.

LEVELS OF LANGUAGE LEARNING

Second-language learners pass through four generally recognized stages. The activities in this book are designed for students in the pre-production and early production phases, but adaptations and enhancements are included for more proficient students, too.

1. **Pre-Production Phase.** Learners in this phase cannot comprehend simple words and phrases; they lack basic English vocabulary and knowledge of grammar. This stage is also known as the "silent period," since learners may appear withdrawn and shy. Though silent, they are absorbing language all around them and processing it in their own time.

2. **Early Production Phase.** Students in this phase use basic vocabulary in one- to two-word sentences, and begin to follow basic grammar patterns. They may struggle in conversation, but they are beginning to understand what people are saying to them.

3. **Speech Emergence.** Students show greater independence in this phase. They may struggle to elaborate upon ideas, but they speak in longer phrases and understand most of what is said.

4. **Intermediate Fluency.** Learners speak and comprehend most classroom discourse. They may still struggle with complex grammar and pronunciation, but they can initiate and extend conversations comfortably. Academic areas, such as content reading in science or social studies, still present challenges.

WHAT IS PROFICIENCY?

There are two types of language proficiency (Cummins, 1980). Though they often overlap, each type involves distinct sets of skills. Second-language learners develop both proficiencies simultaneously, and one can enrich the other.

Basic Interpersonal Communication Skills (BICS) is the ability of second-language students to communicate socially with native English speakers. Students with these skills can talk on the telephone and in the playground, for instance, and play group games. This proficiency is often achieved within six months to two years after arrival in a new country. Since language learning is inherently social, and being able to communicate is a prime motivator for learning a second language, children will be especially busy with these skills during their first year.

Cognitive Academic Language Proficiency (CALP) is the ability of second-language students to learn academic subjects in English and to handle the language demands of the grade-level curriculum. Students with this skill can understand and use advanced vocabulary, follow complex written instructions, make logical arguments, compare and contrast, persuade, describe, summarize, and comprehend reading in content areas. This takes five years or more to develop fully.

Using This Book

This book is divided into two parts that are both designed to give your second-language learners basic literacy experiences.

PART 1 INCLUDES:

• **Tips for Welcoming Your New Students.** The first section of this book includes pointers for preparing for your students' first days and weeks, assessment tools for understanding your students' level of English, a list of the National Standards, and suggestions on how to involve and welcome the students' families.

PART 2 INCLUDES:

• **Mini-Books.** As your students work on these books, they gain early literacy experience (the text is patterned and predictable, with strong visual cues) and writing practice (in some books, students copy the text onto each page). At the same time, they begin to build their confidence ("I made and read a book cover to cover!").

• **Picture Dictionary Pages.** Interactive pages that focus on building a basic vocabulary.

• **Games.** Fun and easy games for new students to get to know their classmates.

In Part 2 you will find activity instructions, adaptations for enhancing the language skills introduced in the unit, and cross-curricular links. This section also includes suggestions on how to involve families. Each unit includes:

• **Make a Mini-Book.** Directions for completing the section's mini-book. A writing prompt or activity is often included to help students expand on a theme as they develop their writing skills. For instance, students may complete various writing activities, continue the mini-book using the pattern provided, and/or write new books on the same theme.

• **Art.** These projects build language skills and help students express themselves non-verbally. Since art projects are process-oriented, they are also key opportunities for simple narration: "I am cutting the paper. Now, you are gluing the scraps on."

• **Classroom Fun.** This is a teacher-led or small-group game or activity that builds language and provides an opportunity to socialize.

• **Listening Center.** These activities provide ideas for using a listening center in your classroom. Recording the mini-books on tape provides auditory reinforcement and helps students work independently.

• **Word Play.** Idioms that correspond to the theme are included in each unit for more proficient students. Students might illustrate them or depict real-life examples of the idiom.

• **Home Connection.** Activities that encourage family involvement, integration of the home culture into the classroom, and continued development in the first language are included.

• **Book Links.** A list of books that enhance the theme of the unit. The books are visually engaging and feature simple English text to help learners build concepts.

Welcoming New Students

Before your new students arrive, try completing some of these simple projects:

1. Make a "welcome" tape with a bilingual volunteer (a student, parent, or school employee) in the first language of your newcomers. Here are a few ideas for what to include on the tape:
- A warm welcome message to each of your new students
- Name and address of the school
- Reassurance that the teacher and other students will help them learn English
- A brief list of supplies students should bring to school every day
- How to get lunch, catch the bus, find the school office and the nurse
- What to do in case students experience any trouble
- English words, such as "bathroom" and "help"

2. Gather materials and set up a language learning center (page 17).

3. Find out as much as you can about the native cultures of your new students, their language proficiency, and their first-language literacy development. Through your school office, you may be able to get transcripts from their previous schools.

4. Prepare the rest of the group to welcome the newcomers (page 20). You might ask the rest of your class how they would feel if they suddenly moved to another country. (There may be students in the class who have moved to the United States who can help build empathy for your newcomers' situations.) Have children brainstorm ways they might help new students, and have the group complete the "welcome" collaborative book on page 21.

5. Consider seating options. The new students should be surrounded by other students and, if possible, sit next to a child who speaks their language. Some children might feel uncomfortable in the front row center.

The First Few Days

Here are some quick ideas on how to make your new students feel welcome:

1. Make sure you know how to pronounce your newcomers' names. Point to yourself and say, "My name is…" Then point to each new student and say, "What's your name?" Ask the rest of your class to do this, too.

2. Help your new students make an identification card if they don't already have one. They can keep the card in their notebooks, backpacks, or pockets. It should include name, grade, teacher, classroom, language spoken, home address and number, family contact numbers, and a list of other children or adults in the school who speak their language. You might use an index card and include a photo, then have it laminated. This will be helpful if students become lost, but will also help them read and memorize basic information.

3. Give them a copy of "What Should I Say?" (page 60) and have them tape it to their desks or keep in a notebook. Show students how to use the page and fill in the blank spaces.

4. Give students paper, pencils, crayons, and markers, and let them relax and draw at their desks. (They may be so overwhelmed that they shut out all spoken information.) Communicate friendliness, patience, and

warmth with body language and a smile. You might also give them some of the books or textbooks that you will be using that year, so they can browse through them in a low-key, low-demand setting.

5. If possible, have someone who speaks the new students' first language give a school tour, including important places such as the bath-room, nurse, school office, and cafeteria. Make sure they know how to say "bathroom" and "nurse." An English-speaking peer can be a great help with this.

6. Give students a photo of your whole class labeled with students' names. New students will begin to connect faces to names and build a foundation for socializing.

The First Week

• Have bilingual and picture dictionaries on hand. Younger children can benefit from a simple picture dictionary. Students in grades 3 and up should have a children's bilingual dictionary. Help students familiarize themselves with how to use it.

• Involve the rest of your students. Make a weekly schedule (page 50) and an alphabet chart (page 31) so that they have a quick reference at their desks.

• Help your new students get involved. From the start, give new students simple, non-verbal classroom jobs, such as distributing and collecting papers and cleaning the board with a partner. Have other students model exactly what you would like the newcomers to do.

• Help students make a Personal Dictionary. Here's how:
1. Reproduce page 61 about 10–25 times.

2. Cut each page down the middle and help students staple them into a book. (They might want to design and make their own covers from sturdy paper.)

3. Have students write a new word, use it in a sentence, and either illustrate it or give the translation on the line provided.

Uses for the Personal Dictionary.
• Weekly vocabulary test

• Homework (Help students find five key words in that night's homework assignment.)

• Personalized spelling tests

• Creating theme dictionaries (Students choose a theme, such as animals, food, games, sports, or machines, and then list new words related to the theme on several sheets.)

• Alphabetizing exercises (Students put all the words on the page in alphabetical order.)

• Crossword puzzles or word search games (Students create puzzles using new words.)

• Story starters (Students make up a story using all five words on the page.)

Assessing the Needs of Your Newcomers

To get a sense of your students' language skills, choose a private place to work and a time when students seem relaxed. Try the following exercises; each one addresses a different area of language development. These exercises will give you an initial sense of your students' language capabilities. However, day-to-day informal assessment will give you a clearer picture of each student's skills.

Letter Knowledge. Show a copy of the alphabet written in both upper and lower case. Ask students to tell you the letter names and/or sounds each letter makes.

Counting: Share a pile of small objects (pennies, paper clips, marbles, or toys) with each student. Say, "Let's count these. One, two…"

Next, show students these numbers and see if they can name them in English:

   2   4   9   13   50   42   86   75
   100   205   1,000   1,999   5,684

Include a computational math test, using your grade-level math curriculum. (Don't include word problems.)

Speaking. Show students an engaging picture (you might use the "School Picture Dictionary," page 24) showing some sort of action or interaction. Ask, "What is happening here?" "What is this for?" or "What is [subject] doing?" As your students speak, notice the words they use, pronunciation, grammar patterns, tenses, subject–verb agreement, the time it takes to get the idea across, and their comfort level.

Listening Comprehension. Ask the following questions and give the following commands. Record students' responses (only one word or a nod from a student is necessary):

Questions:
• Can you speak English?
• Can you read and write in English?
• What is your name?

• Where are you from?
• How old are you?
• Who are the people in your family?

Commands:
• Stand up.
• Jump.
• Sit down.
• Close your eyes.
• Open your eyes.
• Touch your nose.
• Raise your hand.
• (show a book) Open the book. Close it.
   Next, sit with a box of crayons or markers. Give simple, color-related commands such as "Show me the red crayon." Repeat with each color.

Reading and Reading Comprehension. If the students can read in English, choose a short passage from a book that you regularly use in your class, making sure it falls at the low end of the range of reading difficulty. In turn, ask your new students to read it aloud. Next, ask the students simple comprehension questions using *who, what, when,* and *where*. If a student cannot do this, drop a reading level until you find one where the student is successful.

Writing. If students can write in English, give them pencil, paper, and an eraser. Ask them to write their names, then write about their families, friends, favorite sports, or former schools. Notice word choice, the length of the writing passage, subject–verb agreement, spelling, time it takes to complete the task, and how well the students expressed their ideas.

National Standards

The TESOL (Teachers of English to Speakers of Other Languages) Association has created national guidelines for grades Pre-K through 8. Though children of different ages achieve these goals differently, the goals remain the same across grade levels. Keep these standards in mind as you plan the instruction and assess student progress. You might even create a personalized assessment system for each student based on the standards and include it in their portfolios.

Goal 1, Standard 1
To use English to communicate in social settings. Students will use English to participate in social interactions:
- sharing and requesting information
- expressing needs, feelings, and ideas
- using non-verbal communication in social interactions
- getting personal needs met
- engaging in conversations
- conducting transactions

Goal 1, Standard 2
To use English to communicate in social settings. Students will interact in, through, and with spoken and written English for personal expression and enjoyment:
- describing, reading about, or participating in a favorite activity
- sharing social and cultural traditions and values
- expressing personal needs, feelings, and ideas
- participating in popular culture

Goal 1, Standard 3
To use English to communicate in social settings. Students will use learning strategies to extend their communicative competence:
- testing hypotheses about language
- listening to and imitating how others use English
- exploring alternative ways of saying things
- focusing attention selectively
- seeking support and feedback from others
- comparing non-verbal and verbal cues

- self-monitoring and self-evaluating language development
- using the primary language to ask for clarification
- learning and using language "chunks"
- selecting different media to help understand language
- practicing new language
- using context to construct meaning

Goal 2, Standard 1
To use English to achieve academically in all content areas. Students will use English to interact in the classroom:
- following oral and written directions, implicit and explicit
- requesting and providing clarification
- participating in full-class, group, and pair discussions
- asking and answering questions
- requesting information and assistance
- negotiating and managing interaction to accomplish tasks
- explaining actions
- elaborating and extending other people's ideas and words
- expressing likes, dislikes, and needs

Goal 2, Standard 2
To use English to achieve academically in all content areas. Students will use English to obtain, process, construct, and provide subject-matter information in spoken and written form:
- comparing and contrasting information
- persuading, arguing, negotiating, evaluating, and justifying
- listening to, speaking, reading, and writing about subject-matter information
- gathering information orally and in writing
- retelling information
- selecting, connecting, and explaining information
- analyzing, synthesizing, and inferring from information
- responding to the work of peers and others
- representing information visually and interpreting information presented visually

- hypothesizing and predicting
- formulating and asking questions
- understanding and producing technical vocabulary and text features according to content area
- demonstrating knowledge though application in a variety of contexts

Goal 2, Standard 3

To use English to achieve academically in all content areas. Students will use appropriate learning strategies to construct and apply academic knowledge:
- focusing attention selectively
- applying basic reading-comprehension skills, such as skimming, scanning, previewing, and reviewing text
- using context to construct meaning
- taking notes to record important information and aid one's own learning
- applying self-monitoring and self-corrective strategies to build and expand a knowledge base
- determining and establishing the conditions that help one become an effective learner (e.g., when, where, and how to study)
- planning how and when to use cognitive strategies and applying them appropriately to a learning task
- actively connecting new information to information previously learned
- evaluating one's own success in a completed learning task
- recognizing the need for and seeking assistance appropriately from others (e.g., teachers, peers, specialists, community members)
- imitating the behaviors of native English speakers to complete tasks successfully
- knowing when to use native-language resources (human and material) to promote understanding

Goal 3, Standard 1

To use English in socially and culturally appropriate ways. Students will use the appropriate language variety, register, and genre according to audience, purpose, and setting:
- using the appropriate degree of formality with different audiences and settings

- recognizing and using standard English and vernacular dialects appropriately
- using a variety of writing styles appropriate for different audiences, purposes, and settings
- responding to and using slang appropriately
- responding to and using idioms appropriately
- responding to and using humor appropriately
- determining when it is appropriate to use a language other than English
- determining appropriate topics for interaction

Goal 3, Standard 2

To use English in socially and culturally appropriate ways. Students will use nonverbal communication appropriate to audience, purpose, and setting:
- interpreting and responding appropriately to nonverbal cues and body language
- demonstrating knowledge of acceptable non-verbal classroom behaviors
- using acceptable tone, volume, stress, and intonation, in various social settings
- recognizing and adjusting behavior in response to nonverbal cues

Goal 3, Standard 3

To use English in socially and culturally appropriate ways. Students will use appropriate learning strategies to extend their sociolinguistic and socio-cultural competence:
- observing and modeling how others speak and behave in a particular situation or setting
- experimenting with variations of language in social and academic settings
- seeking information about appropriate language use and behavior
- self-monitoring and self-evaluating language use according to setting and audience
- analyzing the social context to determine appropriate language use
- rehearsing variations of language use in different social and academic settings
- deciding when use of slang is appropriate

Easing Into English

BASIC SHELTERING STRATEGIES

Sheltering is a broad term that includes many different strategies for providing second-language learners with language they can understand (Krashen, 1982). Here are some basic tips for teaching and communicating with students new to English:

Slow Down

Speak more slowly and pause between sentences. Wait patiently for the student to answer, even if there seems to be a long, uncomfortable silence.

Show and Tell

• **Use props.** If you were teaching a unit on deserts, for instance, a cupful of sand, a handful of rocks, little plastic lizards, a cup of water, and a picture of a cactus would all give students a visual anchor and aid comprehension. Move the objects around to demonstrate your ideas: "Cacti store water" [hide water behind picture] or "Lizards live in the sand" [put lizard on sand]. Let students handle the objects as you say the object's name, and encourage them to repeat names after you.

• **Use visuals.** Pictures, lists, charts, graphs, Venn diagrams, and maps all help students move concepts from the abstract to the concrete.

• **Write it out.** Being able to see words rather than just hear them is one more inroad into learning a language.

Repeat, Repeat, Repeat

Repeat words, sentences, instructions, and questions several times slowly. Students may be concentrating intently on each word and need repetition to put them together.

Pantomime

Act out words, sentences, and ideas. Simple hand movements ("come here," "one minute") can greatly aid comprehension of a more complicated message. Basic messages—"time to eat," "push in your chair," "good work"—can all be communicated with a small gesture. Use games such as role-playing and charades.

You may notice cultural differences in children's understanding of hand gestures. For instance, the U.S. practice of curling the index finger to gesture "come here" or patting the head to show affection may be perceived as rude in some other cultures. You might explain the difference directly or demonstrate the gestures with other children first, rather than singling out the second-language learner.

Use Manipulatives

A shoebox full of small objects can serve several important purposes. It can be a visual-cue box from which you can pull visual references during your lessons. For instance, the sentence "Birds migrate south in the winter" can be acted out with a plastic bird, a calendar, and a small map. You can also illustrate prepositional concepts— use a cloth and a doll to illustrate sentences, such as "He is under [on top of, next to, etc.] the blanket." Manipulatives are perfect for counting or vocabulary practice. You might say, "Count 20 marbles" or "Put the tiger next to the giraffe." You can also provide story starters by putting several of the items in a bag and asking students to pick an object and then write or tell a story involving what they chose.

Here is a sample list of helpful classroom manipulatives: toy people; animals; cars and trucks; marbles in different colors and sizes; a folded cloth; calendar; small map; stamps or coins from a student's country of origin; a box of crayons; and several blocks in various shapes, sizes, and colors.

Preview

• **Pre-teach important vocabulary.** Write five or six key words on paper and illustrate their meaning. When talking about the desert, for example, draw pictures (or use images clipped from magazines) on chart paper next to the words *lizard, sand, cactus, rocks,* and *water.* This will help new-language learners understand the meanings of words more quickly.

- **Preview the lesson.** Have an English-speaking volunteer, who also speaks a new student's language, briefly explain key points from the lesson in the student's first language. For instance, "Deserts have very little water. You might find cactus, lizards, and sand dunes in a desert. In your lesson, you'll learn how plants and animals survive in deserts."

Simplify

- **Choose your words carefully.** Use high-frequency words as much as possible (e.g., choose *fast* over *rapid* or *quick*).
- **Use simple, subject–verb–noun sentences.** Use proper names rather than pronouns to avoid abstraction. For example, "Tomas goes to the store," or "Mikhail runs home."
- **Break down questions.** Simplify your questioning strategies. For instance, "Look at the picture." [Indicate picture; child looks.] "Where is the lizard?" [You might act like a lizard; child points to lizard in picture.] "Is the lizard sleeping or running?" [You imitate both actions; child answers with one word.] Similarly, break down large chunks of information into smaller chunks. For instance, choose three key points that you want students to take away from the lesson. When asking questions, stick with simple *who, what, when,* and *where,* avoiding *why* and *how.*
- **Keep it short.** When reading aloud from a book, keep passages short and check comprehension as you go.

Make It Relevant

When students can relate concepts in English to their own lives, they will likely remember and understand the information. On a world map, for instance, you might point out where the

second-language learners are from and explain, "This is [is not] a desert."

Make It Clear That Mistakes Are Okay

Most children will take risks in a new language only if they feel it's safe to make mistakes. Anxiety, low self-esteem, shyness, perfectionism —all can contribute to the raising of the *affective filter* (Krashen, 1982), the emotional block that hinders learning. When we're stressed, we don't perform as well. When the affective filter is "down," however, language can flow freely to and from the learner. You can help keep the affective filter low by keeping the student's language demands appropriate—difficult enough so that the children are learning, but easy enough as to be achievable. One way to do this is to correct errors indirectly. For instance, if a student says, "Yesterday I make cake," you might respond, "Yesterday you made a cake? Great!"

Work Together

Working cooperatively in small groups (page 14) gives students more opportunity to speak and interact meaningfully with others. Strategies for making small-group work successful include assigning specific roles and giving the second-language learner one challenging yet achievable task, such as labeling certain parts of a picture with simple words.

USING A BUDDY SYSTEM

A friendly face, especially of a child who shares the first language, can make all the difference to a newcomer. Such a buddy can help the newcomer with classroom and school routines and help the new student become a part of the group. Following are some tips and ideas for making buddies work in your classroom:

• Consider the personalities of both students. Also, think about whether such a responsibility would be a burden on the buddy. You might rotate buddies so that no child feels put upon.

• Coach the buddy in ways he or she can best help. Here are some things that the buddy should do: Speak slowly, repeat frequently, be patient, use gestures, and include the newcomer in playground games and after-school events.

• Make a list of the everyday things a new student should know. (Your English-speaking students may be able to help with this.) Consider your daily routine. Include on the list such things as where you hang your coat, store your books, sharpen pencils, get lunch, find the nurse, and catch the bus.

• Make a certificate for each buddy that shows your appreciation for his or her helpfulness and patience.

GROUP WORK

When given the opportunity to have meaningful, small-group interactions with English speakers, second-language students are more likely to communicate in English:

• Give second-language learners specific roles in which they can excel, such as being in charge of supplies, drawing, cutting, folding, and creating charts and timelines.

• Let the newcomer be the teacher. In a cooperative math group, for instance, let the new student teach the rest of the group how to count to ten in his or her first language, or show a new way to solve a problem (computational skills may have been taught differently in the student's country of origin). Having the rest of the group try to repeat the new words

raises awareness on both sides. The group sees how hard it is to learn a new language, and the newcomer sees that other children might be embarrassed trying to pronounce new words, too.

• Challenge the group as well as the newcomers. Set a simple goal for the group. For instance, "Ling should be able to count 10 things in the picture you create together."

• For more proficient learners, the *jigsaw approach* (Aaronson, 1978) is a powerful cooperative technique. In a group activity, assign one part of a learning task to each student, who then works to become the "expert" in that area and reports back to the group.

INVOLVING FAMILIES

Different cultures have different perspectives on family involvement in school. Some parents are eager and willing to visit the classroom and to get involved in various ways, while others are more reluctant. Reasons for this may include discomfort with their English-language skills, a culture of respect for teachers that translates into not asking questions or "favors," or simply an overwhelming schedule as they adjust to the everyday demands of their new situation. So how can you communicate to parents the importance and value of their involvement, volunteer hours, and efforts at home in helping their children succeed in school?

Have an initial conference to welcome the families into school life and find out as much as you can about the students and their home culture. Ask parents to bring a translator to the conference, if possible, or provide one for them. Be aware that extended family members may also attend the conference.

Questions you might ask at a conference:

• What is your child's previous schooling experience?

• What subject did your child enjoy the most?

• What subjects are challenging for him or her?

• Does your child read and write in his or her

first language?
- What does your child like to read?
- Do you read at home with your child?
- How does your child handle frustration? Does he or she enjoy working independently? Is it difficult for your child to ask for help?
- What are your hopes for your child this year?
- Do you have any questions about your child's school experience this year?
- How can I help your child this year?
- What are your expectations regarding your child's English-language development?
- What are your child's hobbies? Favorite sport?
- What is your child good at (sports, music)?
- What motivates your child?
- What are some of your family celebrations?
- How does your family recognize achievement?
- Is there anything special happening in your family right now?
- What special skills and talents do you have? Would you like to visit the class and share these skills with the group?

You might explain certain school practices that may be unique to American schools. Many cultures do not put emphasis on cooperative learning, lively classroom debates, and parent involvement in school. Some cultures place an emphasis on rote memorization of facts. Explain your classroom practices and procedures. You may also want to print a list of defined special terms that are likely to be new to families, such as whole language, learning centers, phonics, invented spelling, cooperative learning, and portfolio assessment. You might also provide them with a list of families with children in your school who speak the same language as they do. (Be sure to get permission before giving out such information.)

Some parents might expect their child to speak English well within a year. It may be helpful to advise that true social and academic proficiency is a much longer process (see "What is Proficiency?," page 5). Explain to parents what can be reasonably expected that year. By the end of one year, for instance, their child will probably understand most spoken directions in the classroom, perform at grade level in certain areas of the math curriculum, read simple texts in English, get his or her basic needs met in English, and have English-speaking friends.

You might also advise parents to:
- Read and speak to their child in their native language. Make it clear to parents that you value bilingualism and continued language development in the first language, as it will enrich their second-language development.
- Encourage children to find real-life reasons to continue writing in their first language, such as writing letters to friends and family in their home country.
- Help their child with homework if they can.
- Ask their child to use their first language to tell them all about their day.
- Help their child get a public-library card so that they may take out books in both their first language and in English.
- Explore the possibility of signing up their child for social, high-interest extracurricular activities, such as scouting, sports teams, karate, or art classes.
- Ensure their child has a quiet, well-lit study space at home, gets enough sleep each night, and eats a good breakfast before coming to school.
- Let their child watch high-quality public-television programs that enhance and enrich second-language skills, such as *Sesame Street, Barney,* children's nature programs, and even question-and-answer game shows (students can benefit from watching *Wheel of Fortune*). Most importantly, advise parents to limit the time children spend watching television, because real interaction is the best way to learn a new language.

Looking at Cultural Differences

CULTURE SHOCK

Culture shock (the phenomenon, coined by anthropologist Kalervo Oberg in 1960, is also referred to as *culture fatigue*) is a psychological reality for newcomer children and can involve anger, anxiety, estrangement, sadness, loneliness, homesickness, and frustration. The emotional trauma of having to function in a completely new cultural environment is often compounded by a set of difficulties that would challenge even the most stable, resilient child. It may help to find out if a newcomer's family fled their country under difficult circumstances (war, poverty, political persecution) and whether they may be experiencing new difficulties in the United States: separation from friends and family, linguistic isolation, or economic worries. Your understanding of the stages of culture shock can ease the child's burden and give you a window into what's happening:

1. **Excitement and euphoria.** Upon arrival in the new country, children and families may feel initial excitement and euphoria.

2. **Shock.** The constant stimuli of new language, places, and faces become overwhelming. At this stage, without the ability to communicate or fully express themselves, children may appear anxious, lonely, scared, or withdrawn.

3. **Comfort and anxiety.** Children begin to move from anxiety to comfort, gradually learning to cope and to recover from the stress of the new culture's demands.

4. **Acceptance.** Children begin to accept and adapt to the new environment, and develop greater confidence in their bicultural identities. Second-language learning is also second-culture learning. Give children the time and understanding they need in order to adjust, and their process of adaptation may go more smoothly.

DEEP CULTURE

We might easily see differences in the language, dress, food, and music of another culture, but *deep culture* involves much more. Think of culture as consisting of various elements: family structure, periods in a person's life, roles of children and adults, discipline, time and space, religion, food, health and hygiene, history, traditions, holidays, and celebrations (Saville-Troike, 1978).

All these areas have important implications for teachers: What kind of teacher–student relationship does the student expect? If a child misbehaves, how will their family perceive the situation? Does the child have any food restrictions? Within the household, what emphasis is placed on timeliness or order? How much personal space is the child accustomed to having? Through parent conferences and your own research, find out as much as you can about the culture and bring this understanding into your interactions with the student.

Language Learning-Center Materials

It doesn't cost much to equip your classroom with a year's worth of supplies for English-language teaching and learning. Some of the most inexpensive, common materials are also the most useful. Here's a list of supplies to help you get started:

WORD GAMES

• **Boggle™** is good for letter recognition, building a sight vocabulary of short words, and teaching blends. ("How many words can you find that start with ST- ?")

• **Scrabble™** assists in spelling, letter recognition, consonant and vowel blends, and even multiplication (double-word score, triple-letter score). The children's version includes picture cues; the adult version has more letter tiles for sorting and counting.

• **Word-search puzzles** are excellent for independent seatwork, and building letter- and word-recognition skills.

INDEX CARDS

Keep the following sets of cards in large self-sealing plastic bags so they don't get mixed up:

• **Silly sentences.** On separate index cards, write three articles (*a, an, the*), 10 adjectives (e.g., *big, red, excited, silly*), 10 nouns (e.g., *boy, dog*, the student's name), 10 verbs (e.g., *went, read, jumped*), and several prepositional phrases (e.g., *over the moon, into bed, on the table*). Use one color for nouns, another for adjectives, and so on. Help students arrange them in a pocket chart (or on their desks) into silly sentences. There are also commercially available magnetic versions of this activity.

• **Synonym sort.** Compile groups of synonyms (e.g., *hot, warm, boiling*, or *cold, freezing, chilly*), writing one word on each index card. Mix up the cards and have students sort synonyms into piles. Useful categories include *good* (e.g., *great, fine, amazing*) and *big* (e.g., *gigantic, huge, enormous*).

• **Opposites.** Write pairs of opposites (e.g., *hot-cold, good-bad*) on separate index cards, and have children match opposites.

• **Sounds the same.** More proficient learners can sort homonyms (e.g., *be/bee, two/too/to*) into piles and use each word in the pile in a different sentence.

• **Concentration.** Write a word on one card and draw a picture on the other (for instance, write "bumblebee" on one and draw a bumblebee on the other). Students play concentration by placing all cards facedown and then turning over cards in sets of two, trying to make a picture–word match (see concentration games on pages 27 and 46).

• **Bingo.** Pre-teach vocabulary sets by cutting index cards into halves or quarters and having children write one new word on each card. Set them out in a five-card by five-card grid (one blank card in the middle). Call out simple definitions (you say, "it flies," and a student places a marker on "butterfly") until a student gets five in a row.

• **Flash cards.** Have older students write a new English word on one side, and the equivalent word in their first language on the other (they can use bilingual dictionaries to do so).

• **Labels.** Help children use index cards to label things in their desk and around the room, such as door, window, shelf, box, and clock (page 23).

PICTURE FILE

Collect photos from old magazines (many families are willing to donate magazines to the classroom) and glue them on strong backing. Gather pictures in broad categories, such as food, animals, weather, sports, and things in school. Label each picture and keep them in separate boxes or envelopes. Once you have a small library of images, learners can play different types of vocabulary-building games. With food pictures, for instance, students might do the following:

• **Express personal preferences.** Students sort the pictures into three piles or large envelopes labeled "like," "don't like," and "my favorite." They can then say or write simple sentences, such as "I like rice. I don't like chicken. My favorite is pizza."

• **Sort and categorize.** Sort pictures into two piles, one of fruits and one of vegetables, for instance.

• **Create open-ended dramatic play scenarios.** Younger children might pretend to go shopping in a supermarket or serve a fancy meal with the images in the file.

• **Invent and tell stories.** Make up a story about what is happening in each picture. (Why is the woman eating the cake so happy? How does the farmer grow so many vegetables? What does the whipped cream say to the strawberries?) You might also give the student three pictures and have them make up a story that involves all three.

• **Answer simple comprehension questions without speaking.** You might ask, "What ingredients do you need to make a cake?" prompting students to pick out pictures of egg, sugar, and flour. "Which is warmer, soup or ice cream?" or "Which is bigger, a blueberry or a watermelon?"

• **Color sort.** Students can sort pictures by color: green vegetables or fruits in one pile, red vegetables or fruits in another, yellow in another.

TAPE RECORDER AND TAPES

A simple tape recorder, headphones, and blank tapes (the shorter the better) can be an invaluable resource to your language learner. Here are some ways to use them:

• **Welcome tape.** Have a "welcome" tape made in your newcomers' first languages and have them listen to it on their first day (page 7).

• **Assessment.** Tape your new students speaking English or reading aloud in the beginning of the year. You might interview them (e.g., "What is your name?" "Where are you from?"). Say the date at the beginning of the tape, and continue to tape at regular intervals throughout the year. Such tapes can serve as assessment tools and be a morale boost for the

learners, who will naturally encounter low points during the year. At the half-way point or end of the year, listen to the tape together to appreciate how much second-language development has occurred.

• **Listen to a book.** English-speaking children or parent volunteers can read books aloud on tape so that second-language learners can follow along. You might add a sound effect, such as a bell or clap, that signals when to turn the page.

• **Listen to a song.** Tape songs that the class knows and sings often in school, so that the learners can begin to memorize them and sing along.

WOODEN BLOCKS

Simple, blank, die-shaped blocks can be made into various language games. You can purchase them at game stores, or you might simply use children's building blocks. Use blank stickers or permanent markers to write on them for the following activities:

• **Math games.** For math-equation practice, make regular dice and talk through math concepts: "What number did you roll?" "What does four plus two equal?" Make a third block into a "symbol" block with "plus," "minus," "divided by," and "times" (include both symbols and words, repeating two symbols), so that students can become familiar with math language.

• **Sentence games.** Use the same concept as "Silly Sentences" under the "Index Cards" section (page 17), but put six different words on the sides of six different blocks.

• **Subject–verb agreement games.** On one block, write *he, she, I, you, we,* and *they* (you might substitute the student's name for *he* or *she*). On another, write *am, are, is, were, was,* and *will be.* Students roll the dice and see if their match is grammatically correct. If so, they make a sentence using the two words. If not, they roll one of the dice over again until they get a match. A third block in this game might include adjectives, such as *happy, tired, sad, hungry, excited,* or *mad.*

Mini-Books, Activities, and Games

USING THE MINI-BOOKS

Mini-books are a powerful tool for second-language literacy development. They are patterned so that students know what to expect, provide strong visual cues that correspond directly to the text, and allow for creativity and a sense of satisfaction.

How to make the mini-books:

1. Make a double-sided copy of the mini-book pages for each student.
2. Have students cut along the dotted lines and put the pages in order, placing page 3 behind the title page.
3. Fold the pages in half along the solid lines.
4. Make sure the book pages are in order, then staple the book along the spine.
5. Invite students to complete their mini-books with crayons, pens, or pencils.

Note: To make the mini-books for "How Many?" (pages 33–34) and "Food Friends" (pages 47–48), make a single-sided copy of the pages for each student. Have students cut apart the panels and place the pages in order.

How to use the mini-books:

- **Work one-on-one.** Sit with the student and read together, pointing to each word as you say it. Point to the pictures that correspond to the text, too. After repeated readings, the student may be able to read the books independently.

- **Give as independent seatwork.** As they use the mini-books on their own, students can look up words they don't know in a bilingual dictionary (for older children) or a picture dictionary (younger children). Students who are very new can simply color the book, working at their own pace. Since the pages are numbered, they can also put them together independently.

- **As part of a listening center.** Second-language learners can tape themselves reading the book (or you might tape yourself or another student). Afterwards, students can listen to the tape as often as they like. This helps students who have not yet begun speaking in English, as well as auditory learners. The combined auditory and visual input (the tape and the book) gives students two entry points into English.

- **Put students in the role of leader.** Once students have mastered the text in a book, they might read to younger students who share the same first language. They might even take the book home and teach new words to their families, especially younger siblings.

- **Teach English concepts of print.** Some languages don't share the same left-to-right, top-to-bottom directionality of English writing. Use the mini-books to help students understand and create English books, teaching words such as *front cover* and *back cover*, *left* and *right*, *top* and *bottom*, and *beginning* and *end*.

- **Build word-recognition and grammar skills.** Write all the text on index cards, one word or sentence per card. Children can reorder the cards as they compare them to their mini-books. This builds sight-word recognition, awareness of sentence structure, and visual memory.

- **Teach phonics in context.** Use the text in the books to teach sound–symbol correspondence and build awareness of the sounds of English: "Red starts with R" [point to the r].

Welcoming the Newcomers

Preparing a group of native English speakers to welcome newcomers to the United States can be a valuable and enriching process. Here are some collaborative book ideas to help children build a sense of community and support for the new students.

MAKE A COLLABORATIVE BOOK

My Name Is... This collaborative book can help build whole-class responsibility for helping newcomers while also helping the new students learn their classmates' names.

Make a copy of page 21 for each student. Engage students in a discussion about the many different ways they might help the newcomers. Give each student a copy of the page and have them write their names in the space provided, then complete the sentence "I can help you ..." Encourage them to illustrate the page. For instance, a student might write, "My name is Mara. I can help you find the right bus." She could then attach a photograph of herself or a drawing of a bus. When everyone has completed their pages, copy the cover ("Welcome to Our Class," page 22) onto construction paper and bind the pages into a book. Present the collaborative book to your new students.

MORE COLLABORATIVE BOOK IDEAS

Encourage your class to create additional collaborative books that will introduce newcomers to their new environment:

Our Town. On a sheet of white paper, write "In [town or city's name], you can _____." Make a copy for each student. Have students fill in something fun to do in your town. For instance, "In San Francisco, you can ride a cable car to Fisherman's Wharf." Encourage students to draw a picture of what they wrote. For the book cover, write the name of your town and state on construction paper. This collaborative book is a way of giving the newcomers a class-made "tour" of their new hometown.

Our School. To familiarize newcomers to places around school, write "This is _____" on a piece of paper. Make a copy for each student, then have students fill in the name of a place or person in the school. For instance, "This is the cafeteria" or "This is Ms. Perez, the principal." Have students illustrate or attach a photograph of whatever they write about. Newcomers might carry this book with them throughout the day so that they begin to connect names with places and faces.

In Our Class. On a piece of paper, write "In our class, you can _____." Make a copy for each student, then have students fill in the blank with a favorite classroom activity. For instance, "In our class, you can draw." Have them illustrate their sentences.

FAMILY ORIGINS

Consider a whole-class unit on family origins, a topic relevant to all students. Themes of immigration, language and cultural differences, and different traditions will inevitably arise. You might also simply post a world map and help students add pushpins to indicate their family's origins.

CULTURE RESEARCH

Before the new students arrive, engage the class in a half-day research project to find out everything they can about the students' home countries and languages. Not only will their findings sensitize them to the newcomers' situation, they will also learn important things about the students' culture (see "Looking at Cultural Differences," page 16).

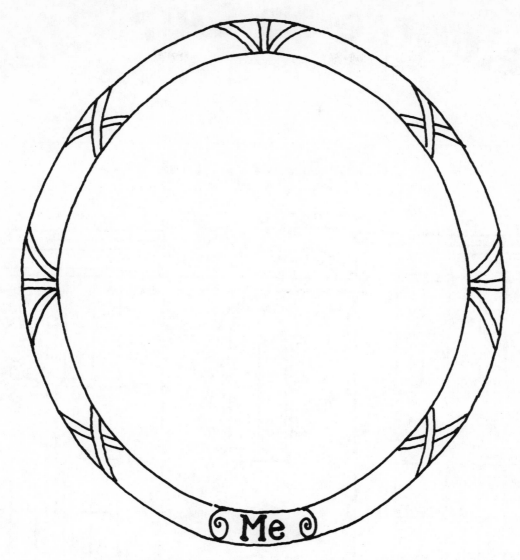

Me

Draw yourself (or glue a photo) here.

My name is _____.

I can help you _____

_____

_____

_____ .

Welcome to Our Class

_____

New Student's Name

At School

Second-language learners will need to know basic vocabulary and how to follow simple classroom instructions. Use the following activities, tips, and mini-books to help them build vocabulary and begin to function in the classroom.

MAKE A MINI-BOOK

At School. Give each newcomer student a copy of the Picture Dictionary (page 24) to study and color. Have students complete the mini-book "At School" (page 25–26), writing the words on the lines below the pictures. Using both the Picture Dictionary and mini-book as reference, students can use colored markers and index cards to label different objects around your room. This will help new students learn the words for many things in the classroom. (You can also use this idea for English-speaking new readers.)

ART

Crayon Rubbings. Take several school-related objects (e.g., scissors, ruler, pencil, paper clip, calculator, spiral edge of a notebook) and cover them with a large sheet of thin white paper. Give children crayons and let them rub the paper until the objects show through. Encourage them to label the objects.

CLASSROOM FUN

School Concentration. Make two copies of page 27 for each newcomer student. Invite students to color the objects. Then, ask them to cover the pictures and test themselves on the words. Once they are familiar with many of the words, they can cut apart the cards. To play concentration, have students put all the cards facedown, then turn over two at a time to make a match.

What's Missing? Take five small objects found in the classroom, such as a pen, eraser, pencil, paper clip, and piece of paper. Make sure students know the objects' names. (Introduce one object at a time, repeating its name several times.) Let students look closely at the objects for a minute, and then ask them to close their eyes. Remove one item from the group. Ask students to open their eyes and tell you what is missing. Scale down the activity to three objects if all the object words are new to the students.

School Charades. On index cards, write verbs and phrases, such as *sit, stand, read, eat, jump, write, drink, point, open, close, quiet, run, turn the page, line up, raise your hand*, and *turn in your paper*. Model each action first. Then break the whole class into small groups to play School Charades using the words and phrases on the index cards.

LISTENING CENTER

Have students listen to the welcome tape you made earlier (see page 7). You might also read aloud into a tape recorder some of the books listed in Book Links (below) so that students can begin following along independently.

HOME CONNECTION

Students can take their mini-books home to make an "At Home" version of the "At School" mini-book. They might want to use a bilingual or picture dictionary to help them.

BOOK LINKS

I Spy School Days by Jean Marzollo (Scholastic, 1995). Rhyming riddles and detailed photographs of school scenes; useful for any age.

This Is the Way We Go to School: A Book About Children Around the World by Edith Baer (Econo-Clad, 1999). An international look at going to school, with rhyming text.

School Picture Dictionary

Clock

Flag

Calendar

Map

Board

Door

Chalk

Book

Cubbies

Eraser

Shelf

Pencil

Paper

Desk

Book bag

Notebook

Teacher

Glue

Ruler

Crayons

Scissors

Pen

Chair

AT SCHOOL

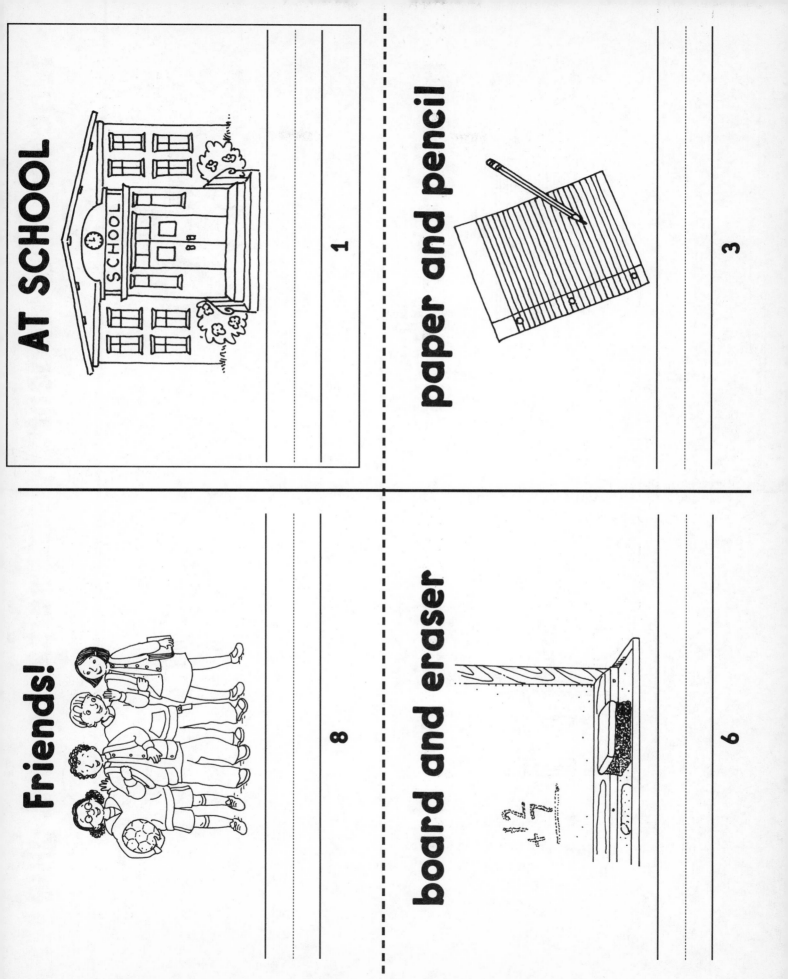

1

paper and pencil

3

Friends!

8

board and eraser

6

teacher and student

scissors and glue

2

notebook and book

4

7

chair and desk

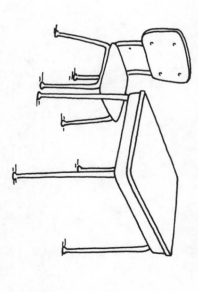

5

School Concentration Cards

student	teacher	scissors	crayons	clock
book	notebook	friends	map	calendar
desk	chair	paper	pencil	glue

ABC's

A strong foundation in letter recognition and letter–sound correspondence provides learners with successful early literacy experiences.

MAKE A MINI-BOOK

As a warm-up for making their mini-books, have students practice writing each letter of the alphabet on page 31. When they're finished, cut the top portion of the page along the dotted line and tape it securely to their desks.

My Alphabet Book. Have students color and assemble "My Alphabet Book" (pages 29–30), and practice writing each letter on the lines provided. Encourage students to make their own alphabet book, one letter per page, and illustrate it. Over time, they might add words that begin with each letter, so that each book page features a list. More proficient students can choose a theme (e.g., food, animals) or write a book with alliterative sentences (e.g., "Annie ate apples").

ART

Alphabet Soup. Cut a sheet of butcher paper or chart paper into a soup-bowl shape and invite children to stamp letters on it with letter stamps or sponges. When they are finished, point to one letter and say its sound. Have children circle that letter in the bowl. Repeat until the entire alphabet has been covered.

CLASSROOM FUN

Lots of Letters. Give students a full set of Scrabble™ tiles to alphabetize.

Eat the Letters. For children unfamiliar with the alphabet, use alphabet cookie cutters (available through school-supply catalogs or toy stores) to make letter cookies. You can also use the cookie cutters on sliced bread or cheese slices.

Big and Little. Use 52 index cards to write out one set of uppercase letter cards and one set of lowercase. Students can play concentration, matching big to little.

LISTENING CENTER

Tape other children singing the alphabet song in different voices: soft, loud, baby voice, deep voice, and so on. Second-language learners can listen to the tape as they read their mini-books.

HOME CONNECTION

If a new student's first language does not use the Roman alphabet, invite a family member to teach the class how to write some simple words using the new student's alphabet, or to sing his or her language's version of the alphabet song.

BOOK LINKS

Alphabet books provide a rich opportunity to teach sound-symbol correspondence and build vocabulary.

Chicka Chicka Boom Boom by B. Martin Jr. and J. Archambault (Simon & Schuster, 1991)

Eating the Alphabet: Fruits and Vegetables from A to Z by Lois Ehlert (Harcourt, 1993)

26 Letters and 99 Cents by Tana Hoban (Greenwillow, 1987)

Alphabears: An ABC Book by K. Hague (Henry Holt, 1999)

Alligators All Around by Maurice Sendak (HarperCollins, 1962)

Animalia by Graeme Base (Abrams, 1993)

Ashanti to Zulu: African Traditions by Margaret Musgrove (Dial, 1992)

From Acorn to Zoo: And Everything in Between in Alphabetical Order by Satoshi Kitamura (Farrar Strauss Giroux, 1992)

The Z Was Zapped: A Play in 26 Acts by Chris Van Allsberg (Houghton Mifflin, 1987)

MY ALPHABET BOOK

AaBbCcDdEeFfGg
HhIiJjKkLlMmNnOo
PpQqRrSsTtUuVvWw
XxYyZz

by _____

1

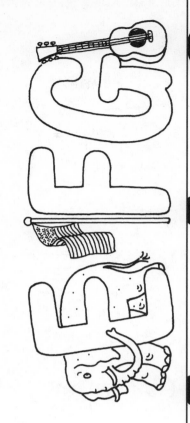

E   F   G

3

Now I know my ABC's, next time won't you sing with me?

Draw yourself here.

8

Q R S T U V

6

A B C D

2

H I J K

4

W X Y Z

7

L M N O P

5

Aa Bb Cc Dd Ee Ff Gg Hh Ii Jj Kk Ll Mm
Nn Oo Pp Qq Rr Ss Tt Uu Vv Ww Xx Yy Zz

A _____   a _____   N _____   n _____

B _____   b _____   O _____   o _____

C _____   c _____   P _____   p _____

D _____   d _____   Q _____   q _____

E _____   e _____   R _____   r _____

F _____   f _____   S _____   s _____

G _____   g _____   T _____   t _____

H _____   h _____   U _____   u _____

I _____   i _____   V _____   v _____

J _____   j _____   W _____   w _____

K _____   k _____   X _____   x _____

L _____   l _____   Y _____   y _____

M _____   m _____   Z _____   z _____

Numbers and Counting

Being able to count and do grade-level math in English can help build a new student's confidence. Since most languages share the same numeral system as English and since math is a less language-demanding area, many students can ease into math right away. These activities and references can help them do so.

MAKE A MINI-BOOK

How Many? Make a copy of the "How Many?" mini-book (pages 33–34) for each student. Have students cut the panels apart, placing the pages in sequential order before stapling them into a book. Encourage students to count the children in each panel and practice writing the number words in the space provided. Students may later want to make their own counting books. Have them use "Numbers and Math Words" on page 35 for reference.

ART

My Money. To make play money, copy money bills in different denominations onto white paper and cut them apart. Students can color them all shades of green. You might want to cover the presidents' faces before you copy the bills so students can draw self-portraits, creating their own currency. Students can play math or counting games with the bills.

CLASSROOM FUN

Make Dominoes. Photocopy the dominoes on page 36. (For a longer game, make extra copies.) Have students color each domino a different color (one color per domino) and cut apart the dominoes along the dashed lines. Students can form a domino chain, matching dominoes with the same numbers. You might also have students match numbers or colors. If they match both, they get a point. Have students play with an English-speaking partner who can model questions using numbers and colors. ("Do you have a red five?" or "I need a blue two.")

LISTENING CENTER

Make a tape that puts counting to music. For instance, sing "one two three four five six seven, eight nine ten and then eleven" to the tune of "Twinkle Twinkle Little Star." More proficient learners can benefit from the "Schoolhouse Rock" math songs, available on tape and CD.

WORD PLAY

With more advanced students, share idioms related to numbers. They might act out or illustrate a scenario that reflects the idiom.

- **Easy as one, two, three**
- **One-track mind**
- **Two peas in a pod**
- **Two-faced**
- **Four corners of the earth**
- **Give me five (high five)**
- **Six of one, half a dozen of another**
- **Behind the eight ball**
- **On cloud nine**
- **Dressed to the nines**
- **Touch something with a 10-foot pole**
- **Eleventh hour**

HOME CONNECTION

Encourage students to make a mini-book with their family that explains the money system in their native country. They can follow the format of the "How Many?" mini-book and present it to the rest of the class.

BOOK LINKS

Anno's Counting Book by Mitsumasa Anno (HarperCollins, 1986). This wordless book contains detailed illustrations; good for all ages.

From One to One Hundred by Teri Sloat (Puffin, 1995). Rich illustrations help students learn to count to 100.

HOW MANY?

by _____

How many?

One _____

How many?

Two _____

How many?

Three _____

How many?

Four _____

How many?

Five _____

How many?

Six

How many?

Seven

How many?

Eight

How many?

Nine

How many?

Ten

How many people are in your family?

_____

_____

Draw a picture of your family here.

Numbers and Math Words

Numbers

1 one	15 fifteen	29 twenty-nine
2 two	16 sixteen	30 thirty
3 three	17 seventeen	40 forty
4 four	18 eighteen	50 fifty
5 five	19 nineteen	60 sixty
6 six	20 twenty	70 seventy
7 seven	21 twenty-one	80 eighty
8 eight	22 twenty-two	90 ninety
9 nine	23 twenty-three	100 one hundred
10 ten	24 twenty-four	200 two hundred
11 eleven	25 twenty-five	300 three hundred
12 twelve	26 twenty-six	1,000 one thousand
13 thirteen	27 twenty-seven	10,000 ten thousand
14 fourteen	28 twenty-eight	

Math Words

$=$ equals $+$ plus $-$ minus $\times$ times or multiplied by $\div$ divided by

$1 one dollar

$5 five dollars

$10 ten dollars

$20 twenty dollars

$50 fifty dollars

$100 one hundred dollars

quarter

dime

nickel

penny

Dominoes

All About Me

Being able to share basic autobiographical information, refer to physical characteristics, and express personal likes and dislikes are all important for second-language learners.

MAKE A MINI-BOOK

All About Me. Invite students to bring in photos of themselves and help them make the "All About Me" mini-book (pages 39–40). Students can interview a friend and make another book based on them. Other mini-book ideas include "My Life Story," which would include stories that reflect important events in the students' life, or "My Home Country," in which students can use maps and photos.

ART

Self-Portraits. Invite students to complete the "Parts of the Body" sheet (page 38). Next, have students take turns tracing each other on large pieces of butcher paper. Students can then cut out the outlines of their bodies and draw life-size self-portraits, labeling each body part. Introduce more advanced vocabulary, such as eyelash, eyebrow, chin, and forehead.

CLASSROOM FUN

Simon Says. Playing games that require non-verbal responses allows students to demonstrate comprehension without having to speak. You might integrate numbers into the game as well (e.g., "Simon says, 'Show me four fingers.'").

LISTENING CENTER

Have students read their "All About Me" mini-books into a tape recorder and listen to it again and again. If they are not speaking yet, read it for them so that they may listen and internalize the language patterns.

WORD PLAY

Share idioms related to body parts with more advanced students. They might write them on the corresponding body part of their life-size self-portraits.

• Butterflies in my stomach
• Big head
• I'm all ears
• Keep a straight face
• Green thumb
• Two left feet
• Knock-kneed
• Heart of gold
• On your toes
• Head and shoulders above the rest
• Cost an arm and a leg
• Apple of my eye
• See eye to eye

HOME CONNECTION

Encourage students to share their mini-books with their families. Together, they might make an "All About My Family" book.

BOOK LINKS

Two Eyes, a Nose and a Mouth by Roberta Grobel Intrater (Scholastic, 2000). Photos of men, women, and children from all over the world, along with simple rhyming text, teach the parts of a face.

The Human Body: A First Discovery Book by Sylviane Perols, Gallimard Jeunesse (Scholastic, 1996). This interactive book with a magic paper flashlight is appropriate for older readers who are ready to explore the human body in detail.

Parts of the Body

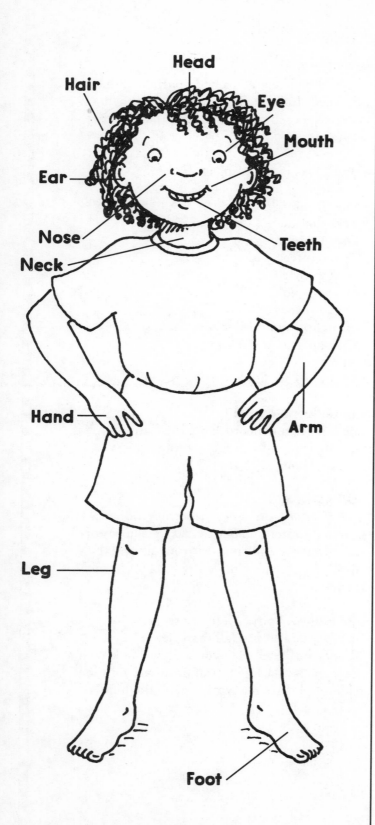

Hair
Head
Eye
Mouth
Ear
Nose
Teeth
Neck
Hand
Arm
Leg
Foot

Draw yourself.
Copy the words.

ALL ABOUT ME

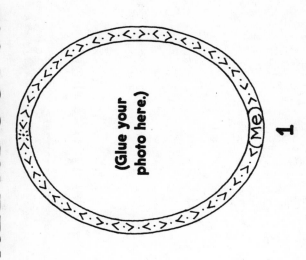

(Glue your photo here.)

Me

1

I am from _____.

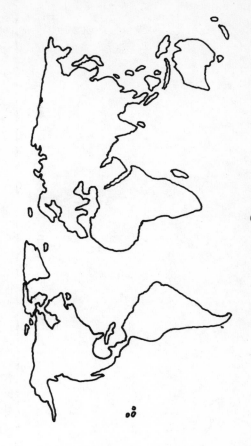

3

Nice to meet you!

(Draw yourself again.)

8

This is my family.

(Draw your family here.)

6

My name is

(Draw yourself here.)

_____ .

2

I live at

_____
(street)

_____
(city, state)

(Draw your house, apartment, or street.)

4

I'm in grade _____ .

(Draw your class or classroom.)

7

I am _____ years old.

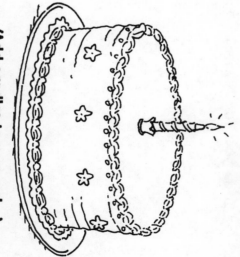

(Add candles to your cake.)

5

Colors and Shapes

Once students know how to use words for colors and shapes, their expressive vocabulary will be greatly enhanced. Use these activities to build and enrich language.

MAKE A MINI-BOOK
Make a Rainbow. To prevent initial frustration as they learn the words for specific colors, give students no more than 10 crayons or markers in basic colors. Make a color label by writing the name of each color in its color on a separate piece of paper (write the word "red" in red). Next, invite students to complete the "Make a Rainbow" mini-book (pages 43–44). As children learn the names for different colors, have them fill in the blanks in the following pattern to create their own color poems:

What is red?
_____ is red. _____ is red.
_____ is red. _____ is red.
Red.

ART
Color Clay. Give students play dough in red, yellow and blue, and let them sit with their "Make a Rainbow" mini-book. Start by taking a little red and a little blue dough and say "Red [hold up red] and blue [hold up blue] make purple [squish the two colors together]." Let the children choose two colors and help them narrate their color creations just as you did. Add white dough to teach "light" and "lighter."

Color the Shapes. Make a copy of "Color the Shapes" (page 42) for each student. Help them read the directions and color the shapes.

CLASSROOM FUN
Eye-Color Survey. Encourage second-language learners to conduct an eye-color survey among their classmates. They can make an eye-color chart by gluing small, colored-paper circles (representing different eye colors) to a piece of construction paper.

LISTENING CENTER
Gather paint samples from a paint or hardware store and have children sort them into their own labeled groups. Have them listen to a taped version of *My Crayons Talk* (see Book Links), and sort color samples according to the taped segment they are hearing.

WORD PLAY
Share idioms related to colors with more advanced students. They might act out or illustrate a scenario that reflects the idiom.

• **Turned pink**
• **Green with envy**
• **Golden opportunity**
• **The grass is always greener**
• **Feeling blue**
• **Red tape**
• **Red carpet**
• **Black sheep**
• **Every cloud has a silver lining**

HOME CONNECTION
Copy the recipe below, adding rebus symbols. For instance, show a rectangle next to "one stick of butter."

Rainbow Cookies
Mix 1 1/2 cups sugar, 1 stick butter, 1/2 cup shortening, and 2 eggs together. Add 2 3/4 cups flour, 2 tsp. cream of tartar, 1 tsp. baking soda, and 1/4 tsp. salt. Shape into balls and roll in colored sugar or sprinkles. Bake 8–10 minutes at 400°.

BOOK LINKS
Of Colors and Things by Tana Hoban (Mulberry, 1996). Colors, shapes, and familiar nouns are presented in a puzzle adventure.

My Crayons Talk by Patricia Hubbard (Henry Holt, 1999). Each crayon in the box has something to say in this rhyming book.

Color the Shapes

circle   square   triangle   diamond   rectangle   oval

Color the circles red.
Color the squares blue.
Color the triangles green.
Color the diamonds orange.
Color the rectangles purple.
Color the ovals yellow.

MAKE A RAINBOW!

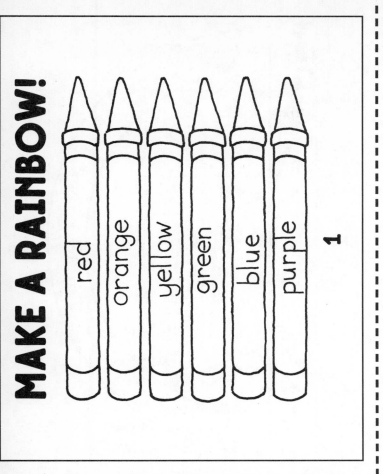

red
orange
yellow
green
blue
purple

1

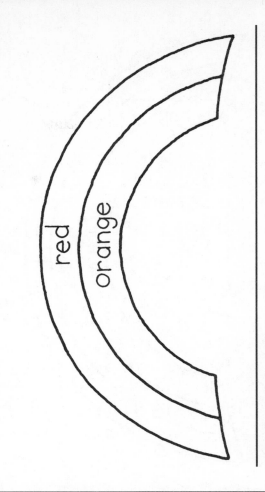

red
orange

orange

3

Make a rainbow!

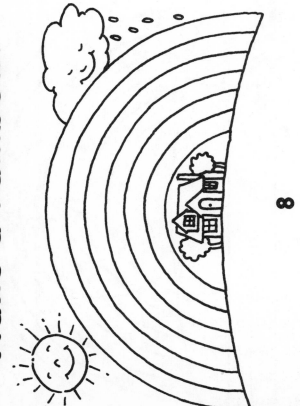

8

red
orange
yellow
green
blue

blue

6

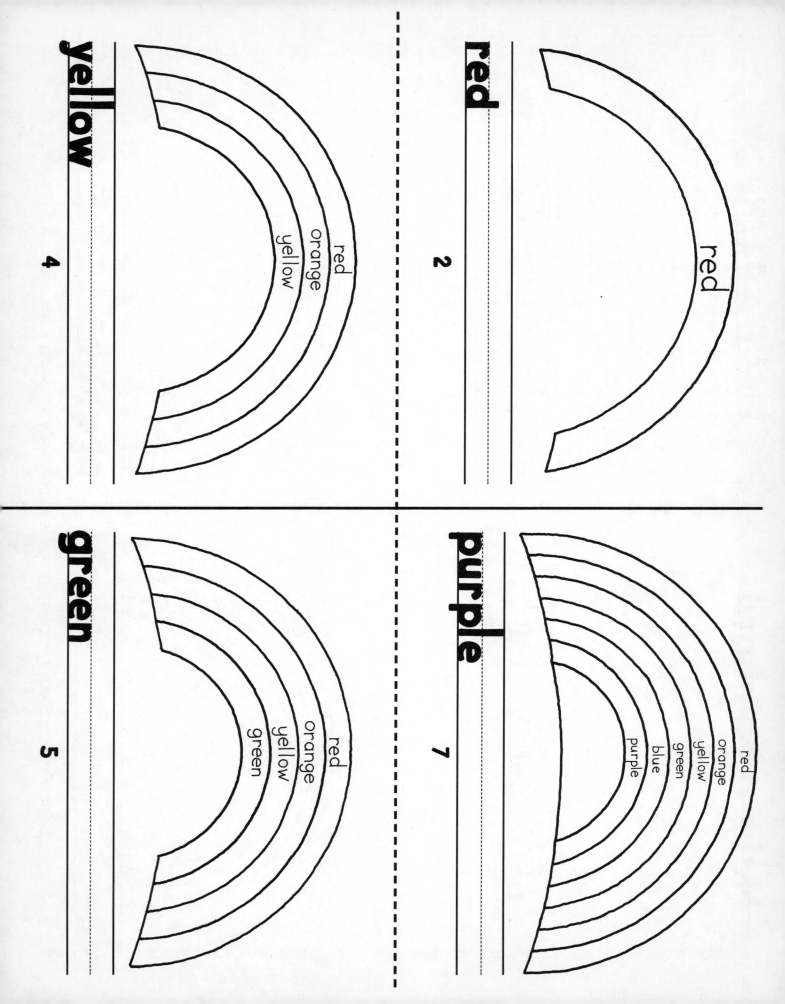

red

2

red

yellow

4

red
orange
yellow

purple

7

red
orange
yellow
green
blue
purple

green

5

red
orange
yellow
green

Food

With a basic vocabulary of food words, students will be able to satisfy their primary needs as well as carry concepts of nutrition over to their second language.

MAKE A MINI-BOOK

Food Friends. To assemble the "Food Friends" mini-book (pages 47– 48), have students cut the panels apart and put the pages in order before stapling together. Encourage students to read the finished book with a buddy. The buddy reads the first word on each page (e.g., "bacon") and the second-language learner completes the phrase (e.g., "... and eggs").

ART

Food Group Murals. Gather old food magazines and invite students to make food-group murals —a poster of fruits, one of vegetables, grains, proteins, dairy, and so on. Next, have students use a picture or bilingual dictionary to label each picture with a sticky note. Invite students to make a dream grocery list, too.

CLASSROOM FUN

Grocery List. Have students use play money and the poster from above to play supermarket. Your second-language student ("customer") names what he or she wants on the poster and an English-speaking student ("cashier") says how much it will cost (e.g., "Thirty cents, please.") The customer gives the money, then the two reverse roles.

Food Concentration. Make two copies of the Food Concentration Cards (page 46). Glue the pages to a piece of tagboard, then cut out the cards to play food-group concentration.

LISTENING CENTER

The mini-book will help build readers' confidence. Have students tape themselves and listen to the book over and over again.

WORD PLAY

Share food-related idioms with more advanced students. They might act out or illustrate a scenario that reflects the idiom. Display their work on a bulletin board covered in an old tablecloth.

- **Walking on eggs**
- **Top banana**
- **The big apple**
- **Apple of my eye**
- **Bring home the bacon**
- **Too many cooks spoil the broth**
- **Life is a bowl of cherries**
- **Don't cry over spilled milk**
- **You can't have your cake and eat it, too**
- **Butter someone up**
- **Baloney!**
- **Nuts about …**

HOME CONNECTION

Invite your new students to bring a special recipe from home. They might bring in a holiday favorite, a special family treat, or a traditional food from their country of origin. The students can teach the rest of the group how to make the recipe.

BOOK LINKS

Bread, Bread, Bread by Ann Morris (Mulberry, 1993). Photographs and simple text explore how bread is eaten and enjoyed all over the world.

I Scream, You Scream: A Feast of Food Rhymes by Lillian Morrison (August House Little Folk, 1998). Tongue twisters, chants, and limericks explore all kinds of food.

The Kids' Multicultural Cookbook by Deanna F. Cook (Williamson, 1995). A great resource for in-class cooking.

Food Concentration Cards

banana	grapes	orange	apple
hamburger	pizza	popcorn	sandwich
carrot	onion	salad	tomato
corn	peas	bread	rice
spaghetti	chicken	eggs	fish
ice cream	milk	cheese	plate
fork	spoon	knife	napkin

FOOD FRIENDS

1

bacon and eggs

2

cereal and milk

3

hamburger and french fries

4

spaghetti and meatballs

5

peanut butter and jelly

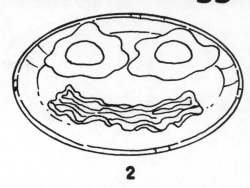

6

rice and beans

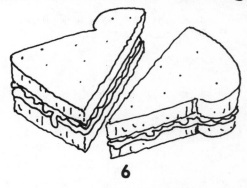

7

bread and butter

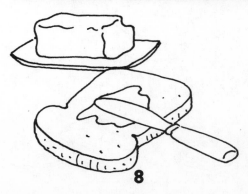

8

peas and carrots

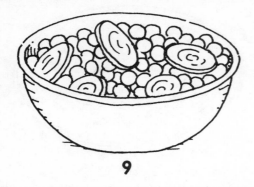

9

salad and dressing

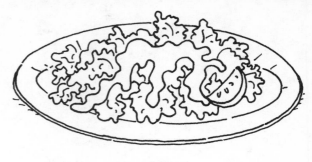

10

turkey and stuffing

11

chips and salsa

12

bagel and cream cheese

13

pie and ice cream

14

milk and cookies

15

Food friends: Me and you!

16

Time and Date

Understanding and using words related to time, date, a daily schedule, months, and seasons can help anchor new students to a routine.

MAKE A MINI-BOOK
Eating Around the Clock. Help students make and read the "Eating Around the Clock" mini-book (pages 51–52).

Next, make copies of the schedule grid (page 50) and help newcomer students make a weekly schedule. This way, they can see what to expect each day. In the space at the bottom of the schedule for each day, write things students need to remember for the next day, such as sneakers for gym class, a permission slip for a field trip, or extra money for the school fair.

ART
Make a Calendar. Use the calendar template on page 53 to help students make their own yearly calendars. Make 12 copies of the page for each student. Provide students with a model calendar and art supplies to decorate each month and write in the months and days. You might teach them to count to 30 or to name the days of the week. Help them write in important days, such as birthdays, holidays, and class events.

CLASSROOM FUN
Calendar Counting. To help students learn the days of the week and months of the year, provide large index cards (seven for days of the week, 12 for months) and write the name of each day or month in pencil. Have students trace over the word using markers. Encourage them to decorate the card, depicting a daily schedule (gym), event (school play today), or holiday (Presidents' Day, school closed) on a corresponding day or month. Shuffle the cards and challenge students to put them in order. More advanced learners can make sentences ("Today is…," "Tomorrow will be…," "Yesterday was…," "The spring months are...," or "Two more months until…").

LISTENING CENTER
Provide students with a play clock and a reading of the mini-book "Eating Around the Clock" on tape. Help them manipulate the hands on the clock as they listen to the book. Once students can tell time well, you might tape instructions, such as "Turn the clock to 3:30 or 12:00."

WORD PLAY
Share idioms with more advanced students and have them illustrate or act out a scenario that reflects the idiom.

- **March comes in like a lion and goes out like a lamb.**
- **Dog days of summer**
- **Fresh as a daisy**
- **Spring chicken**
- **Time flies**
- **Waste time**
- **Rome wasn't built in a day**
- **The last minute**
- **Watch the clock**
- **Around the clock**
- **First thing in the morning**

HOME CONNECTION
Invite children to bring in calendars in their native language. Have your class compare how the calendars are similar and different. Students might also take home the calendar template to make a bilingual calendar with their families.

BOOK LINKS
Take Off With Time by Sally Hewill (Raintree/Steck-Vaughn, 1996). Contains photos of different kinds of clocks, and uses numbers and words to explore the concept of time. Includes a template for a make-your-own clock.

Chicken Soup With Rice by Maurice Sendak (HarperCollins, 1991). This classic introduces the months of the year.

_____'s Week

Monday	Tuesday	Wednesday	Thursday	Friday
Remember!	Remember!	Remember!	Remember!	Remember!

EATING AROUND THE CLOCK

1

At two o'clock (___ : ___)
the worm ate two tomatoes.

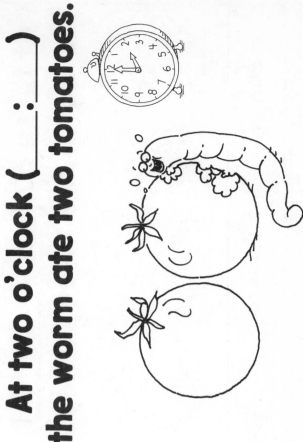

3

Six-thirty (___ : ___)
is dinnertime!

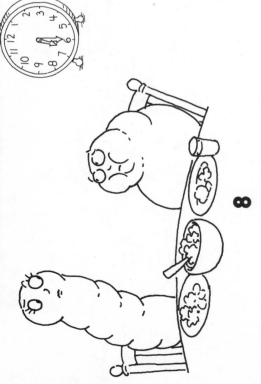

8

At five o'clock (___ : ___)
the worm ate five fries.

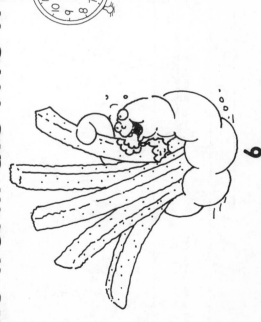

6

At one o'clock (___ : ___)
the worm ate one orange.

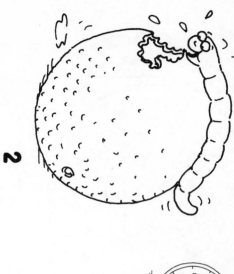

2

At six o'clock (___ : ___)
the worm ate six sandwiches.

7

At three o'clock (___ : ___)
the worm ate three turkeys.

4

At four o'clock (___ : ___)
the worm ate four figs.

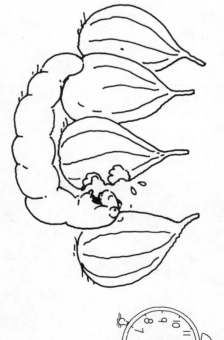

5

_____

month

Sunday	Monday	Tuesday	Wednesday	Thursday	Friday	Saturday

Living in the U.S.A.

As students adjust to their new environment, there are celebrations to enjoy, comparisons to make, and songs to sing!

MAKE A MINI-BOOK
Help students complete the mini-books "The Pledge of Allegiance" (pages 55–56) and "This Land Is Your Land" (pages 57–58). As a writing-extension activity, have students make a list of their favorite things about living in the United States. Have them make another one of their least favorite. Students might also start sentences with "It is different here because…"

ART
Wave Your Flag. Copy the flags reproducible (page 59) for each newcomer student. Help them count the stars and stripes on the U.S. flag and color the flag. Then, have them draw the flag of their country of origin. Next, ask students to make a U.S. flag and the flag of their home country to share with the class. Provide them with a variety of materials: construction paper, paint, shiny star stickers, a star rubber stamp, crayons, markers, scissors, and glue.

CLASSROOM FUN
Cross-Country Road Trip. Write each state's name on an index card. Working with a small group, divide the pile so that each child has a small stack of states. Put a large map of the United States in the middle and challenge the students to "travel" from coast to coast using their cards as tickets. When you say "California," for instance, the student with the California card puts it down on the map. If students have a bordering state (Nevada, Arizona, or Oregon) they may put one of these states down. Continue until there is a line of cards stretching coast to coast. You can play by starting on either the West or East Coast or from a northern or southern state.

LISTENING CENTER
Ask an English-speaking student to help you record the mini-books in this section on tape. Let new students listen to the tapes as they make their books. For "This Land Is Your Land," you may also want to get a musical recording and invite your whole class to sing along. Help new students rewrite "This Land Is Your Land" to be about their country of origin. Encourage them to pick several important or favorite places in their home country (for instance, "From the Black Sea to my favorite playground…"), then record their version of the song.

WORD PLAY
Share some "American" idioms with more advanced students. You might also teach them the simpler state nicknames (e.g., The Lone Star State, The Sunshine State).

- Big Apple
- Windy City
- American as apple pie
- The red, white, and blue
- Old Glory
- White House
- Melting pot

HOME CONNECTION
Have students ask their families to relate the route they took to the United States. The next day, with the help of a map, students can describe the route to the class in English. ("We left Moscow on a plane. We stopped in Germany and changed planes. We flew to New York and got in a taxi.")

BOOK LINK
I Read Signs by Tana Hoban (William Morrow & Co., 1987). A bright, simple introduction to the signs children see in their new surroundings.

THE PLEDGE OF ALLEGIANCE

1

to the flag

3

for all.

(Draw yourself and your friends or family here.)

8

one nation, under God, indivisible,

6

I pledge allegiance

2

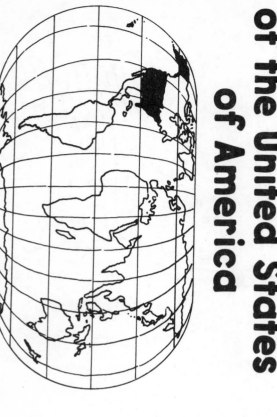

of the United States
of America

4

with liberty and justice

and to the Republic for
which it stands:

5

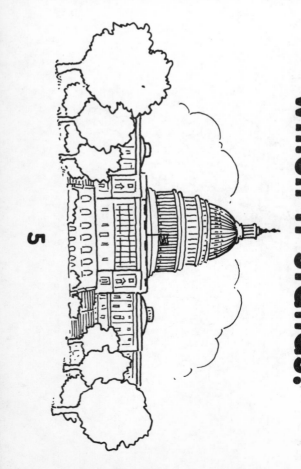

7

THIS LAND IS YOUR LAND

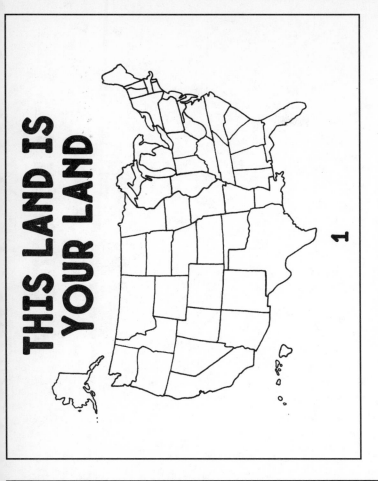

1

This Land is My Land

(Draw yourself.)

3

This Land was made for You and Me.

(Draw yourself with your friends or family.)

8

From the Redwood Forests

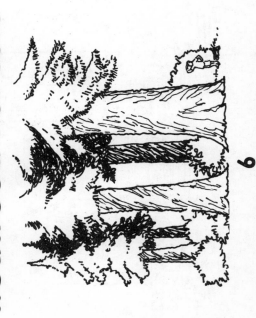

6

This Land is Your Land

(Draw a friend.)

2

From California,

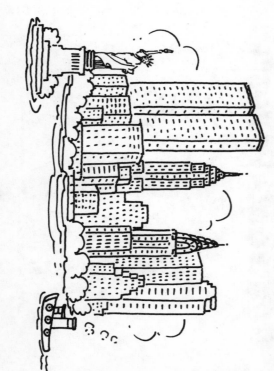

4

To the Gulf Stream Waters,

7

To the New York Island,

5

The Flag of the United States

Color every other stripe RED. Leave the other stripes WHITE.

Leave the stars WHITE, too. Color around the stars BLUE.

The Flag of My Native Country: _____

(Draw your flag here.)

What Should I Say?

Translate these sentences into your native language.

I don't speak English.

_____

I speak a little English.

_____

Can you help me?

_____

I need a _____.

_____

I have a question.

_____

I know the answer.

_____

Can you speak slower, please?

_____

Can you repeat that?

_____

What does _____ mean?

_____

How do you say _____?

_____

I don't understand.

_____

Can you show me, please?

_____

I know the answer, but I can't say it in English.

_____

I understand.

_____

This is too hard.

_____

This is too easy.

_____

May I use the bathroom?

_____

May I get a drink?

_____

Where are we going?

_____

I don't feel well.

_____

My Personal Dictionary   Date: _____

1. _____

2. _____

3. _____

4. _____

5. _____

My Personal Dictionary   Date: _____

1. _____

2. _____

3. _____

4. _____

5. _____

Classroom Resources

NEWCOMER LIBRARY

These books address the special experiences of children new to the United States. Clear visual cues and simple text will aid students' comprehension and help them feel that they are not alone in their experience. If a book is too advanced for an individual learner, you might read it aloud to the group so that the newcomer can pick out the basic themes.

America the Beautiful by Katharine Lee Bates (Atheneum, 1993)

Angel Child, Dragon Child by Michele Surat Surat (Scholastic, 1989)

Anno's Journey by Mitsumasa Anno (Paper Star, 1997)

Anno's USA by Mitsumasa Anno (Paper Star, 1998)

Call Me Ruth by Marilyn Sachs (Willam Morrow & Co., 1995)

Children of the River by Linda Crew (Laurel Leaf, 1991)

Coming to America: The Kid's Book About Immigration by David Fassler, Kimberly Danforth (Waterfront Books, 1993)

Everybody Cooks Rice by Norah Dooley (The Lerner Publishing Group, 1991)

Hello, Amigos! by Tricia Brown (Henry Holt, 1992)

Hoang Anh: A Vietnamese-American Boy by Diane Hoyt-Goldsmith (Holiday House, 1992)

How My Family Lives in America by Susan Kuklin (Simon & Schuster, 1992)

I Hate English! by Ellen Levine (Econo-Clad, 1992)

In My Father's House by Ann Rinaldi (Econo-Clad, 1999)

Journey to America by Sonia Levitin (Atheneum, 1993)

Orphan Train Rider: One Boy's True Story by Andrea Warren (Houghton Mifflin, 1996)

The Long Way to a New Land by Joan Sandin (HarperTrophy, 1986)

The Star Fisher by Laurence Yep (Puffin, 1992)

Train to Somewhere by Eve Bunting (Houghton Mifflin, 2000)

Yang the Youngest and His Terrible Ear by Lensey Namioka (Yearling Books, 1994)

CD-ROMS

Independent computer work with CD-ROMS can be a great source of language development. There are several excellent resources for second-language learners. Here are a few:

I Spy series (Scholastic) is rich in rhyme, visual cues and new vocabulary.

Arthur's Reading Race (Creative Wonders) is a "living book" that involves environmental print and allows students to construct their own sentences.

Chicka Chicka Boom Boom (Simon & Schuster) is a wonderful musical and visual introduction to the Roman alphabet.

Usborne's Animated First Thousand Words (Scholastic), an interactive picture dictionary, is a comprehensive vocabulary-building resource.

USEFUL WEB SITES

http://www.everythingesl.net is a comprehensive resource for all teachers working with second-language learners.

http://eslgames.com has games for second-language learners.

http://www.tesol.com is the Web site for the Teachers of English to Speakers of Other Languages Association.

http://www.nabe.org is the Web site for the National Association for Bilingual Education.

http://www.eslmag.com is an online ESL magazine.

http://www.etanewsletter.com is a newsletter for English as a Foreign Language teachers.

http://www.teachers.net has chat rooms for teachers of second-language learners.

BIBLIOGRAPHY OF PROFESSIONAL DEVELOPMENT BOOKS

Asher, J., *Learning Another Language Through Actions*. Los Gatos, CA: Sky Oaks Productions, 1996.

Baicker, Karen, *Immigration: Then and Now*. New York, NY: Scholastic Professional Books, 1997.

Claire, Elizabeth and Haynes, Judie, *Classroom Teacher's ESL Survival Kit #1*. Englewood Cliffs, NJ: Alemany Press, Prentice Hall Regents, 1994.

Claire, Elizabeth, *ESL Teacher's Activities Kit*. Upper Saddle River, NJ: Prentice Hall Trade, 1998.

Cummins, J. ,*Model for the Empowerment of Minority Students: Implications for Teacher Education*. Washington, D.C.: National Clearinghouse for Bilingual Education, 1992.

Ford, Claire Maria, *101 Bright Ideas: ESL Activities for All Ages*. Reading, MA: Addison-Wesley Publishing Co., 1996.

Igoa, C., *The Inner World of the Immigrant Child*. New York, NY: St. Martin's Press, 1995.

Garcia, E., *Understanding and Meeting the Challenge of Student Diversity*. Boston, MA: Houghton Mifflin, 1994.

Glasscock, Sara, *Read-Aloud Plays: Immigration*. New York, NY: Scholastic Professional Books, 1999.

Haynes. Judie, *Newcomer Program: Activity Copymasters & Teacher's Guide*. Englewood Cliffs, NJ: Alemany Press, Prentice Hall Regents, 1997.

Krashen, S., *Principles and Practices in Second-Language Acquisition*. Oxford: Pergamon Press, 1982.

Richard-Amato, P.A., *Making It Happen: Interaction in the Second-Language Classroom*. New York, NY: Longman, 1988.

Saville-Troike, M., *A Guide to Culture in the Classroom*. Rosslyn, VA: National Clearinghouse for Bilingual Education, 1978.

Smallwood, Betty Ansin, *The Literature Connection: A Read-Aloud Guide for Multicultural Classrooms*. Reading, MA: Addison-Wesley Publishing Co., 1989.

Tiedt, P.L. & Tiedt, I.M., *Multicultural Teaching: A Handbook of Activities, Information, and Resources*. Boston, MA: Allyn & Bacon, 1990.

Vilot, J. Harris, ed., *Teaching Multicultural Literature in Grades K-8*. Norwood, MA: Christopher-Gordon Publishers, Inc., 1992.

The Kids' Book of the 50 Great States: A State-by-State Scrapbook Filled With Facts, Maps, Puzzles, Poems, Photos and More! New York, NY: Scholastic Professional Books, 1998.

Wong Fillmore, Lily, "When Learning a Second Language Means Losing the First," *Early Childhood Research Quarterly*, 6(3), 323–346, 1991.

Congratulations!

_____
Student's Name

You came to a new school and started learning a new language.

You listened to and spoke English every day.

You began to understand a new country.

You didn't stop trying!

For all these things, you should be proud.

You made it!